PIGS OVER COLORADO

I ♥ COLORADO

Kerry Lee MacLean

On the Spot! Books

PIGS OVER

Dear Readers,
 This story is about my five children and the real-life vacations we've taken all around our home state, Colorado.

This is Andrew Piggy.

This is Sophie Piggy.

This is Gregory Piggy,

This is Tessa Piggy.

WELCOME TO ROCKY MOUNTAIN NATIONAL PARK

COLORADO

(This is our guardian piggy.
He makes sure we don't get lost.)

PSSST! LOOK FOR
5 DIFFERENT COLORADO
ANIMALS HIDING ON
EVERY PAGE!

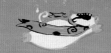

and this little piggy's name is Kelly.

BOULDER

TOWN

DENVER
Elitches

COLORADO
SPRINGS

PUEBLO

AL GORGE
RIDGE

AMOSA

*great blue heron, wolf, great horned owl, river otter, great egret

N
W E
S

SPRING
The Great Sand Dunes

During spring vacation, we sky-piggies like to cruise down south to the Great Sand Dunes and roll around in the warm, slippery sand. Sophie does long jumps. Andrew hunts for sidewinders - and finds one! Tessa flies up to the top of the tallest dune. Gregory uses his magnet to pull iron out of the sand and saves it in a bag. Kelly, the actress, just strolls along the crests of the dunes looking like a movie star.

Royal Gorge Bridge

On the way back from the sand dunes we cross the highest suspension bridge in the world. It's *over 1,000 feet tall!* After checking to make sure no one is below, Gregory tosses pebbles off the bridge. Kelly counts how long it takes each one to hit. Tessa reminds them that it's against the law to throw anything off the bridge, even little pebbles. Andrew catches a sagebrush lizard. He takes a good look, then lets it go on it's way. Poor Sophie gets a *little* dizzy!

*collared lizard, ravens, pallid bat, ring tail, pinon mouse

Dinosaur National Monument

Sometimes we fly out west to visit the dinosaurs that used to live here. Andrew spots a living distant relative of the dinosaurs on the wall right above him. Sophie takes rubbings for her school report. Kelly

measures the biggest fossil she can find. Tessa looks for a brachiosaurus bone. Gregory's imagination gets the best of him!

SUMMER
Colorado River

When the summer starts heating up, we sky-piggies *love* whitewater rafting down the Colorado River! We need the biggest, strongest piggy to guide the boat, so Andrew sits up front. Since Sophie's

YUMMY!

sharp eyes never miss a thing, her job is to be the lookout for dangerous rocks ahead. Gregory and Tessa sit in back, laughing every time we hit a rapid. Kelly just hangs on for dear life!

*kingfisher, bald eagle, vultures, coyote, rainbow trout

Mesa Verde

A trip Southwest to see these eight-hundred-year-old apartments is lots of fun, especially if we go before it gets too hot! Sophie and Kelly explore the back of the cave. Gregory loves all the hidden passageways. He sneaks around pretending to be a spy from another tribe. Tessa imagines she can see the Anasazi performing a sacred ceremony in the kiva.

— ISN'T IT A LITTLE DARK IN HERE?

Lucky Andrew finds a perfect arrowhead,
but it's sharper than he thinks!

Maroon Bells

Hiking in the Rockies is fun. We see all kinds of strange animals and colorful flowers. Tessa makes it to the top first so she puts a stone on the cairn. Andrew points out the 14,000 foot Maroon Bells mountains. Sophie can't go one step further without water. Kelly helps. Gregory thinks he hears a mountain lion!

*marmots, mountain lion, least chipmunk, red squirrel, white-crowned sparrow

FALL
Estes Park

    With our tartan caps and bagpipes, we're ready for the Scottish Festival in Estes Park! Tessa loves dancing. She joins the eightsome reel. Kelly leads the parade as "Nessie", the Loch Ness Monster from Scotland. Sophie, who happens to be a very good cook, helps with cooking the haggis. ('Haggis' is a Scottish specialty of sheep's heart and liver mixed up with scotch and oatmeal, stuffed in a sheep's stomach and boiled!) Gregory, the musician, plays "Long Live the Queen" on the bagpipes. And, like a good, true Scotsman, Andrew bravely eats his haggis!

Denver

Denver has all kinds of fun, but our favorite is Elitch's all lit up at night! Gregory, the maniac, goes for the fastest, scariest rides! Andrew does the bungee jump! Sophie pigs out on cotton candy, Dot's Ice-Cream-of-the-Future and funnel cakes with warm chocolate sauce.

*magpie, barn owl, garter snake, gray squirrel, robin

Kelly tries the Twister II. Tessa wishes she hadn't!

Boulder

    Since we're in the neighborhood, Sophie, the expert climber takes us rock climbing on the Flatirons high over Boulder. She's so light on her feet, she climbs faster than the deer that live here. Andrew shows off for the pretty piggy below - just in case she's watching him. Gregory stops to dig for mica. Tessa belays so no one will get hurt. She's especially worried about Kelly who likes climbing a little *too* much! And, sure enough, Kelly swings out on the rope like a total maniac!

WINTER
Ghost Towns

   In winter, the ghost towns are especially ghostly. About the only thing alive here are snowshoe hares and vultures. Gregory, the detective, finds an antique bullet half-buried near a gravestone and wonders what happened here a hundred years ago... Could it have been a shoot-out over gold?

Tessa hears a strange creaking sound coming from behind her. Phew! It's only a long-tailed weasel. Discovering a crooked old pan, Sophie tries her luck at panning for gold - she spots something shimmering beneath the sand and gravel. Andrew explores every building, looking for clues about the gold miners. Kelly isn't so sure she wants to land here after all!

*snowshoe hares, elk, turkey vulture, long-tailed weasel, dark-eyed junco

Breckenridge

Tessa, the artist, gets us to enter the Breckenridge Snow Sculpture Competition. She cuts a magnificent Statue of Liberty out of a mountain of snow. Kelly can't believe how big it is! Gregory smooths the whole surface. Sophie pours everyone hot chocolate with gooey, melting marshmallows. They all work hard, but Andrew is the biggest help of all!

*badger, red fox, peregrine falcon, water pipit, bobcat

Vail

We've waited so long for this. Off we go to Vail for the best skiing in the world! Feeling brave, Kelly tries the double black trails. Gregory isn't so sure she's ready...
Sophie spots a famous movie star.

Andrew wins first place in the snowboarding contest! And Tessa, well, she does her best!

*pocket gopher, white-tailed ptarmigan, black bears, rosy finch, gray jay

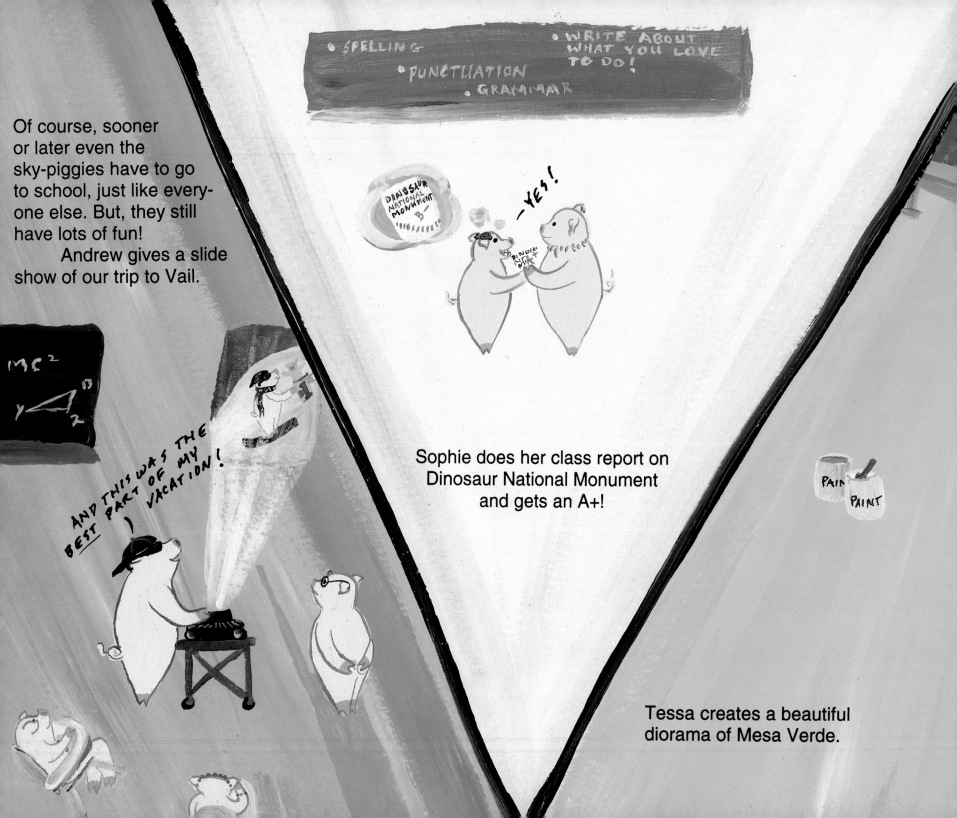

Of course, sooner or later even the sky-piggies have to go to school, just like everyone else. But, they still have lots of fun!

Andrew gives a slide show of our trip to Vail.

Sophie does her class report on Dinosaur National Monument and gets an A+!

Tessa creates a beautiful diorama of Mesa Verde.

Gregory brings his magnet and the huge bag of iron he pulled out of the sand dunes.

Kelly shares her photo album and remembers all the fun they've had on their vacations in Colorado!

FOR THE GOOD + NOBLE FATHER OF ALL THE SKY-PIGGIES, HECTOR HECTOR MACLEAN III. WITH ALL MY LOVE, Kerry TESSA. ♡

SPECIAL THANKS TO KELLY MACLEAN, AMY NICOLSON KIDA, LELAND &

Published by On the spot! Books
1492 Tipperary Street
Boulder, CO 80303

Printed in Hong Kong, ISBN 0-9652998-1-3

The pictures in this book were painted with acrylic paints.

To order more PIGS OVER COLORADO or PIGS OVER BOULDER books,
call, fax or write us at 303-666-0550 (ph/fax), On the Spot! Books, 1492 Tipperary Street, Boulder, CO 80303